Skills for OU Study

D1556044

Preparing Assignments

The Open University Walton Hall, Milton Keynes MK7 6AA

Edited, designed and typeset by The Open University.

Printed in the United Kingdom by Thanet Press.

ISBN 978-0-7492-1265-0

1.1

Skills for OU Study

Preparing Assignments

Writing good assignments may not come naturally to any of us but you will find useful guidance and tips here. This booklet accompanies the *Skills for OU Study* website http://www.open.ac.uk/skillsforstudy, which contains advice, quizzes and exercises to help you improve your assignments.

Contents

1 Types of assignment

University courses differ in the types of assignment required. You could be asked to complete any of the following.

- Essays
- Reports
- Oral assignments
- Short-answer assignments
- Computer-marked assignments
- End-of-course assessments

We describe each of these briefly below but your course materials will give you a much better idea of what is required from you.

> ❝ I feel I'm putting myself up just to be shot down. I'm really exposing my weaknesses. ❞

You may feel a little lost when faced with your first assignment but don't worry, you are not expected to perform perfectly right from the word go. You will have to be patient and you can expect your skills to improve over time.

1.1 Essays

Essays have an introduction, a body and a conclusion. Each of these has a different function.

Essays have an introduction, a body and a conclusion. Each of these has a different function.

The introduction (around 5–10 percent of the word count) should outline the main subject of your essay, identify what your main argument will be and indicate the stages of your argument. Restating the question title in some way is often a good way of outlining your subject, as is highlighting any major issues that are involved.

The body of the essay (around 80–90 percent) is where you set out your main argument. It should have a narrative flow that highlights the sequence of the different points in your argument. Your reader should be able to follow a coherent and continuous 'story' from start to finish.

The conclusion (around 5–10 percent of the word count) should summarise the issues you have raised in the body of your assignment and tie up any loose ends in your argument. It should emphasise the key elements of your argument and it's often a good idea to make reference once again to the question title.

1.2 Reports

Reports are broken up into discrete sections. Check your course materials for advice on the type of report that is required and the sections you need to include.

Reports are broken up into discrete sections that vary according to the type of report you are asked to write. Some types of report may require all of these sections. For other types of report you might not need to include a methodology section, for example. You should check with your tutor and your course materials for details on the type of report and the sections you need to include.

The sections of a report

- Title
- Abstract (or executive summary)
- Introduction
- Methodology
- Results (findings)
- Main body (discussion)
- Conclusions
- References and acknowledgements

The abstract is a self-contained, brief summary of the report, describing its scope and main findings. This is written last as you need to complete the work that you do on the report before you can adequately describe it.

The introduction gives the purpose and scope of the report and there is often a set way of writing it. Outline the aim of the investigation or experiment and list the objectives or intended outcomes. Your introduction should also provide background information to clarify why the investigation was undertaken. Conclude your introduction with a sentence that leads into the body of your report.

The methodology section, where required, is used to describe each step of the research you conducted. For example, did you conduct interviews or experiments, and if so with whom? How did you measure your results?

The results section describes the findings of your research in a clear and concise way. Don't go into the implications of your findings here; that is covered in the main body of your report. Tables, graphs and diagrams are useful ways in which to present quantitative findings.

The body of your report may be broken into sub-sections, which you might want to number. There may be particular requirements

The body of your report may be broken into sub-sections, which you might want to number.

regarding how you order the information in the body of your report for your course. It may be presented:

- in chronological order
- as a statement of the problem, followed by an analysis of possible courses of action and ending on a recommendation
- as the pros and cons for a particular proposal followed by the recommended action.

In your report, you will be expected to discuss your findings in detail by analysing and interpreting your results.

However you organise the body of your report, you will be expected to discuss your findings in detail by analysing and interpreting your results and explaining their significance.

The conclusion should be brief – it serves to sum up the main points of your report in the same way as it would in an essay-style assignment. No new information or points should appear in your conclusion.

1.3 Oral assignments

Oral assignments are used in language courses, where you are expected to record yourself speaking in the foreign language you are studying. Making notes to refer to when you record your submission will help you. However, it is important to keep your delivery natural and to avoid the monotonous result that comes from reading directly from a script. Try to use notes as an aide-memoire rather than a script, just glancing at them from time to time to refresh your memory and have some phrases ready, such as: first of all, secondly, by contrast, to conclude.

Write up or down arrows above those parts of a sentence where your voice should rise and fall – the intonation pattern.

Highlight key words or those you find difficult to say, and underline or highlight the particular parts of unfamiliar words or phrases to show where the stress or emphasis falls. For example, in English:

emphasis, pattern

and in French:

touristes, table

Make your notes simple enough and your writing large enough to follow easily. Complex or detailed notes in small writing are difficult to use. Notes are more useful than full sentences.

Practise speaking your responses for the assignment before you record your voice. Make sure that you state your name, course, your Personal Identifier (PI) number and the time length of the presentation on the recording. Always check afterwards that the whole of your presentation has been successfully recorded.

Practise recording with different volumes, to find out which volume setting works best and how far from the microphone you need to be while you record.

1.4 Short-answer assignments

These assignments, or parts of assignments, are broken into several sections, each of which requires a short and succinct answer. The length of the answer required could be anything from 30 words to 500 words.

Short-answer questions are designed to test your:

- knowledge and understanding of ideas and facts; or

- skills in applying a particular process to data or information.

It is easy to overshoot word limits in short-answer assignments by including irrelevant information. Remember to be concise.

It may seem easier to provide short answers than long essays, but it is just as important to read the question carefully and to take account of the process words (see Section 3.2). It is all too easy to wander away from the subject matter, and to overshoot word limits by including irrelevant information. Remember to be concise, keep to the point and stay within the word limit.

As your answer will be short, there will be less of an emphasis on the structure of your answer, however, you should try to write a full explanation rather than a series of bullet points.

The question set may involve manipulating some given data. This may be mathematical formulae or equations or chemical information. You should demonstrate the thinking behind your answer, rather than simply giving the answer. This will involve showing the logical steps you have taken on the way to achieving your answer.

Diagrams, tables and graphs are often used in written assignments and these can be a useful and colourful way of presenting information. They can also help you to keep the word count down.

1.5 Computer-marked assignments (CMA)

CMAs can be just as challenging as other forms of assignment and require a good deal of thought about which answers are correct.

Some courses use computer-marked assignments (CMAs). The questions have multiple-choice answers and you usually mark a box next to the answer you think is correct. Although you are provided with the potential answers you will find that CMAs can be just as challenging as other forms of assignment and require a good deal of thought about which answers are correct.

Multiple-choice questions test your knowledge of factual aspects of the course. The format of the questions may vary. For example, some might ask you to choose a correct statement from a selection of statements. Others might present you with some information, a question based on that information and then a selection of answers to choose from.

As the selection of answers you are given for a question sometimes vary only subtly, it is essential that you read the question carefully. It will contain the information that you need to make the correct choice. However, try not to labour too hard over any question. If you are at risk of working on a question all night long, remember that it might constitute only a small proportion of the overall marks. If you find that you are stuck on a particular question, try leaving it and returning to it later on.

If your course contains CMAs, you should refer to your course materials to find out more about how you may complete and submit your CMAs.

1.6 End-of-course assessments (ECA)

ECAs are used on some courses instead of a traditional examination. The main difference between an examination and an ECA is that the ECA can be completed at your home rather than in an examination hall on a set date. It is sometimes completed at your own pace and so can feel a little like an ordinary assignment. However, because it replaces an examination, you can't pass the course without doing it and your ECA score is one of the main factors used in determining your course result.

ECAs sometimes involve you doing a little research and very occasionally are collaborative.

The arrangements for ECAs vary from course to course so make sure you refer to your course materials for details.

 Visit http://www.open.ac.uk/skillsforstudy/ to find out more detail about the type of assignment you need to write.

2 The stages of planning an assignment

There is no single correct way of writing an assignment. However, there are some common principles and processes that will help keep you on track while you are putting it together (see Figure 1).

Figure 1   The seven stages in planning your assignment.

Different academic disciplines require different types and styles of writing. So always read the assignment handbook or guidelines for your particular course carefully, and ask your tutor if you are not sure about anything.

2.1 Creating your own strategy

Creating your own strategy is all about knowing what the assessment requirements are for the course and deciding what result you want to get. If you know what is required to pass the course, and what is required to get a distinction, then you can decide what is feasible for you. Some students have busy lives and are time-limited. They may therefore decide to do just what is necessary to pass the course.

Some students have busy lives and may therefore decide to do just what is necessary to pass the course. Other students might have more time and want to devote it to doing well in assessments.

Other students might have more time and want to devote it to doing well in assessments.

Check your course calendar for assignment deadlines and start to think about allocating time to the work needed.

If you think you might have problems meeting the deadline for a particular assignment then get advice from your tutor or your regional centre before the cut-off date.

To find out about the rules for submitting assignments, how to manage your time and studies and where your regional centre is go to http://www.open.ac.uk/skillsforstudy/

2.2 Knowing what's needed

Make sure you know what is required from you for each assignment. Look at your course materials to find out what type of assignment you are expected to do.

It may be that your assignment is divided into separate sections, each allocating different marks. Make sure you know what is required of you and that you don't miss anything out. You also need to know what word limit you should keep to, as exceeding the word limit may lose you marks.

> " I have no idea of where to begin. The last assignment I wrote was when I was at school. "

Take time to understand what the assignment is asking from you.

Take time to understand what the assignment is asking from you. You can discuss any questions you have about the assignment with your tutor, study advisor or your fellow students.

Make sure you keep the assignment task in front of you throughout the whole process from start to finish; keeping your eye on the question will keep you correctly focused.

2.3 Organising what to do

As you gather your notes and relevant course materials, you need to make decisions about what topics and evidence you want to use in your assignment. If you need to include quotes and evidence then make a note of the sources they come from (e.g., books or articles) so you can more easily compile your reference section.

Organise your thoughts by compiling a list or using a mind map to create a plan.

When you are ready to go into the detail of what it is you want to write, try compiling a list or using a mind map to organise your material into a plan. This process helps you to make choices about what needs to be included, what doesn't and which order the points should go in. Plans help you to keep to the question. Try comparing your plan to the assignment task to see if you are still heading in the right direction. Plans also make your drafting process easier as you don't need to keep everything in your head: instead you write it down in your plan. (see Figure 2).

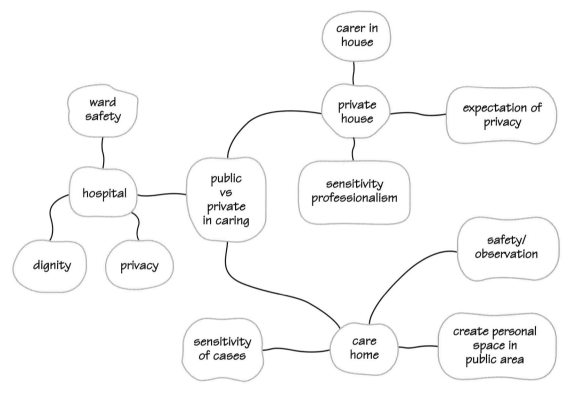

Figure 2   Mind mapping can be a productive way of getting your ideas to flow

When you come up with ideas for your assignment, try not to hold yourself back. Give yourself the freedom to jot down all the words, phrases and names that come to mind. You can always cross them out later on if you change your mind about how relevant they are.

2.4 Drafting

Don't expect to write perfect text at the first go, you will need to spend time going back over and rewriting or reorganising your paragraphs.

First draft

If you are writing an essay, consider how your argument will progress throughout your assignment. Your ideas should lead logically from one to another until you have built the overall thesis of your essay. To do this you need to put the separate ideas that you have generated into a sequence.

Try writing your ideas on the right-hand side of a piece of paper and map each one to a particular part of your essay (see Figure 3).

When you construct your paragraphs, make sure that you:

- describe the idea clearly

- give reasons for its relevance to the essay question

- provide evidence to back up the idea.

The evidence you use to back up your ideas can take the form of direct quotes from books and articles or a simple paraphrasing of someone else's argument or theory. In either case it is essential that you properly reference the evidence you use.

Assignments need a narrative flow. If the main points in your assignment are not linked to one another, your assignment will appear to consist of a list of unrelated points. Knowing how to use linking words and phrases (such as 'however', 'nevertheless', 'consequently') is an essential part of writing for any audience (see Section 5.1).

To see how the mind map in Figure 3 might look in essay form and to find out more about linking words go to http://www.open.ac.uk/skillsforstudy/

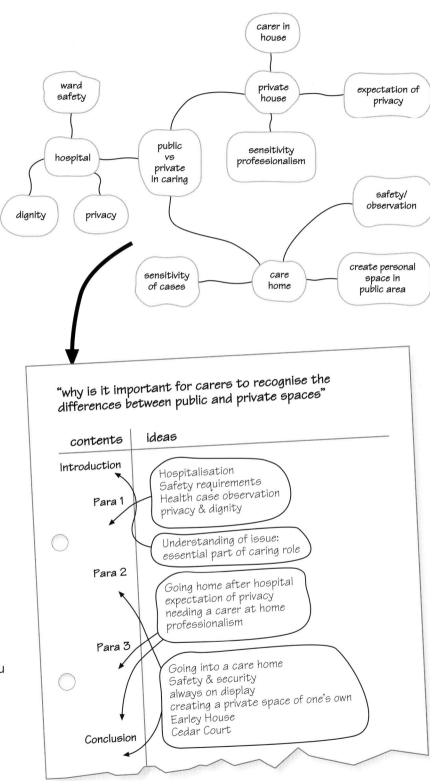

Figure 3   Once you have come up with the ideas you want to write about, you need to sequence them into a logical progression

Second draft

Once you have finished your first draft you may find that a lot of further work might be needed on it. While you go through your second draft stage you need to check the logical order of your argument. You might find that you need to change the order of some points. However, be wary of introducing errors when you do this: although cutting and pasting in a word processor is a handy tool it is very easy to overlook problems with grammar and logic.

At this stage you should also go through your references to make sure that you haven't missed the details of any of your quotes or other supporting evidence.

Finally, an essential part of the drafting process is acknowledging when to let go! It is all too easy to continue to edit your assignment without seeing very much benefit.

2.5 Checking

Once you have finished drafting the content you should check that you have included your name and Personal Identifier (PI) number on every page and that the assignment or question titles are included. Before you print your final clean copy also ensure that the correct formatting is used, for example, 1.5 line spacing (check your course materials for further details) and that the pages are numbered.

Checking your grammar, punctuation and spelling can help you improve your marks.

Although this stage is important you shouldn't spend too much time on checking. Remember to let it go!

2.6 Sending it in

Check your course materials to find out how you are expected to submit your assignment and the cut-off date for its receipt – make sure you allow enough time for it to be delivered.

2.7 Getting it back

This is also an essential part of the assignment process. Part of the purpose of this is to help you improve your skills for the next assignment, so reading the feedback is important.

Although you will first want to see what mark you have achieved, take some time to go through the feedback comments carefully. Identify how you can improve your mark in future. If you have any queries about anything said in the feedback, ask your tutor or study advisor.

Visit http://www.open.ac.uk/skillsforstudy/ to find out more about starting the writing process. You can find out more about how to kick start your thinking, how to craft your writing and decipher assignment questions.

3 Understanding the question

Before you begin to tackle your assignment, you need to make sure that you understand what it is asking you to do.

Every question has key words, and identifying them will help you decide what the assignment is about and what you have to do. 'Content' key words tell you about the topics to be focused on and 'process' words tell what you must do with the content.

First look carefully at the question and identify the key words or phrases.

Every question has key words, and identifying them will help you decide what the assignment is about.

3.1 Content words

Here are some examples of content words in two assignment titles.

> Compare <u>your own education</u> to date with that of <u>one of your parents</u>, <u>one of your children</u> (if you have any) or <u>a friend</u> from a <u>different generation</u>. Which <u>points of comparison</u> seem <u>important</u> to you and why?

> Using <u>examples from the case studies</u> of Jean and Emma in Chapter 5 show how the <u>local environment</u>, including <u>housing</u>, can influence <u>health and well being</u>.

Process words in the question title tell you what you should do with the subject matter. For example, 'compare two theories' or 'justify someone's ideas.

3.2 Process words

These are the words in the question title that tell you what you should do with the subject matter. For example, you might be asked to **compare** two theories or to **justify** someone's ideas. Some of the most common process words are shown in the table below.

Compare	Show the similarities and differences and, perhaps, reach conclusions about which is preferable.
Contrast	Focus on the differences, although you may also note that there are similarities.
Criticise/ Evaluate	Make a judgement (but don't give a personal opinion) about the merit of theories, or opinions, or about the truth of information, backed by a discussion of the reasoning involved and by evidence from the course materials.
Define	Give the exact meaning of a word or phrase. In some cases you may need to give different possible definitions.
Discuss	Explain, then give two sides of the issue and any implications
Explain	Give details about how and why it is.
Justify	Give reasons for a point of view, decisions or conclusions. Also mention any main objections or arguments against.

Here are those question titles again, this time the process words are in bold.

"**Compare** <u>your own education</u> to date with that of <u>one of your parents</u>, <u>one of your children</u> (if you have any) or <u>a friend</u> from a <u>different generation</u>. Which <u>points of comparison</u> seem <u>important</u> to you and **why**?"

"Using <u>examples from the case studies</u> of Jean and Emma in Chapter 5 **show how** the <u>local environment</u>, including <u>housing</u>, can influence <u>health and well being</u>."

As you can see content words are those that contain the 'content' of the question. The process words are those that tell you what to do with the content. Note that there is an implied process word in the final sentence of the first question but the question is essentially asking you to explain why you think the points of comparison you've chosen are important: 'Explain which points of comparison seem important to you and why?'

4 Introductions and conclusions

4.1 Introductions

The length of your introduction should be in proportion to the length of your essay. It should be between five and ten per cent of the total word count. Try to keep to one paragraph, especially if the word limit is under 1000 words. For a longer essay you may write several paragraphs.

Introductions identify the main question or issue.

The function of an introduction is to identify the main question or issue and introduce and define the key words or terms. You should highlight major debates that lie behind the question and signpost the stages of the content or the argument.

You may want to write the introduction before you start, in which case it's a good idea to check and revise the wording for accuracy after you've written the first draft.

For report-style assignments, there is often a set way of writing the introduction. The aim of the investigation or experiment should be outlined, listing the objectives or intended outcomes. You should also provide background information in order to clarify why the investigation or experiment was undertaken and perhaps what you don't intend to write about – thus indicating the scope of your report.

Finish your introduction with a sentence that leads into the body of your report.

4.2 Conclusions

Your conclusion should demonstrate that you have answered the question set for the assignment. You can do this by:

- making reference to the key words (both process and content) in the title

- summarising the key elements of your argument and the main content of the body of your essay or report

- perhaps (especially in a report) suggesting what needs to be considered in the future.

Use your conclusion to demonstrate you have answered the question and to summarise your main points.

Conclusions shouldn't be too long. For an essay or report of fewer than 1,500 words a concluding paragraph of 50–100 is probably sufficient. It shouldn't be longer than the introduction.

Avoid introducing new ideas or examples into your conclusion. Summarise only the main points and don't repeat examples.

5 Writing paragraphs

Paragraphs divide the writing according to topics or major points. Each paragraph should contain one main idea or topic and you should be able to identify what that is. The sentences in a paragraph should contribute individual points to that main idea. Although you may find it difficult at first to distinguish where you should start a new paragraph, you will become better at it over time.

Paragraphs divide the writing according to topics or major points.

The start of each new paragraph indicates a change of focus. Paragraphs sometimes start with a 'topic sentence' to introduce the new focus, and subsequent sentences then expand upon the topic. Sometimes, however, the topic of the new paragraph only becomes clear over several sentences.

Paragraphs can help your reader identify the progression of your argument ... the reader has a visual clue as to when your argument is moving on to the next stage.

Paragraphs can help the reader identify the progression of your argument. When each paragraph contains a new main idea, the reader has a visual clue as to when your argument is moving on to the next stage.

Common mistakes include making each sentence a new paragraph, or, at the other end of the spectrum, having no paragraphing in your writing at all. Poor paragraphing makes it very difficult for your reader to follow your argument (see Figure 4).

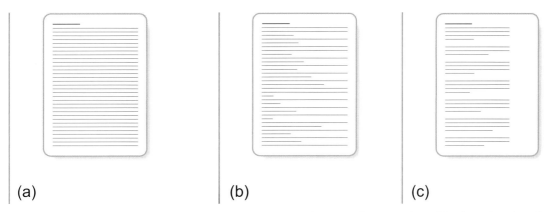

(a) (b) (c)

Figure 4   a) Putting no paragraphs in turns your assignment into one long block and makes it very difficult to read. b) Making every sentence a new paragraph can make your assignment feel like a list. c) A well structured assignment is immediately apparent to the eye.

If you find it difficult to know where to start a new paragraph, try using mind maps to help identify the logical divisions in your argument – they can help you separate your ideas from each other. Making précis notes in the margins of your draft might also help you decide where one idea ends and the next starts.

5.1 Linking words

Linking words help to make your argument flow, and once you have sorted out where your paragraphs start and end, they will help you link those ideas into a coherent whole.

Linking words, such as 'nevertheless' and 'furthermore' can help to make your argument flow.

Linking words remind the reader of the thread so far and provide signposts to what is coming later (see Figure 5). They can be used to

- link ideas in a sentence
- link sentences
- link paragraphs.

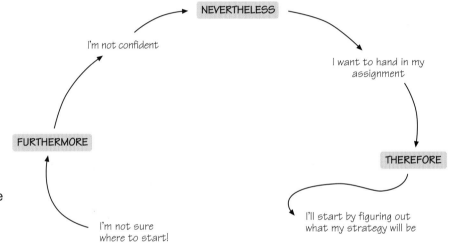

Figure 5
Linking words are an essential part of any writing

Try using some of the following linking words in your next assignment.

To add a point	To contrast two points	To note consequences
and …	but…	because …
also …	However …	as …
In addition …	although …	since …
Similarly …	On the one hand … on the	So …
Not only … but also …	other hand …	Therefore …
Moreover …	Yet …	As a result …
Furthermore …	Nevertheless …	Consequently …
To illustrate, or give an example	**To move on to the next point**	**To summarise or conclude**
for example …	Then …	Finally …
that is …	After this/that …	In conclusion …
namely …	Subsequently …	To conclude …
		To summarise …
		In sum …

6 Paraphrasing, quoting and referencing

Whenever you mention another person's publication, idea or theory, you must acknowledge the source of the material. In your assignments you are usually expected to include information and ideas from your course books. You must never let the reader think that you are claiming the idea or information as your own. If you don't acknowledge the source, and especially if you copy the exact words, you run the risk of being accused of plagiarism.

You'll usually find information about avoiding plagiarism and the style of referencing preferred by your course in your assignment guidelines sent out with your course materials.

Whenever you mention another person's publication, idea or theory, you must acknowledge the source of the material.

6.1 Good habits

You can make writing assignments and avoiding plagiarism much easier by being rigorous in your note-taking habits. While you are reading through your materials, if you take note of a particularly useful quote or if you paraphrase an idea you should also record where it came from. Use the bulleted list below as a guide.

6.2 Referencing

A full reference includes a short in-text reference to each source, with a list of the full details at the end of the assignment. The purpose of a reference is to enable your reader to find the original publication from which you drew your evidence, or upon which you based your argument.

References usually comprise the following information:

- author name and initials
- year of publication
- title of chapter and book (or title of article and journal)
- name of publisher
- place of publication.

The exact format of references varies between academic disciplines and courses so it is a good idea to check your assignment handbook for information on what style of referencing is preferred. One guide is to see how they are handled in your course materials.

6.3 Paraphrasing

Most of your assignment writing will consist of paraphrasing the work of other people. It is a most important skill in academic writing.

Paraphrasing means re-writing someone's argument in your own words.

When you paraphrase someone's argument, you restate their argument but in your own words. You need to make clear that it is someone else's work that you are building upon. You can do this simply by mentioning the author's name, as in the following example, and then listing the full reference details at the end of the assignment.

> Halliday (1978) claims that children develop their language by interacting with those around them.

An important end result of writing ideas or concepts in your own words is that you gain a deeper understanding of the material you are writing about.

6.4 Quoting

If you find that an author has summed up an argument in a particularly convincing way, you may want to quote them directly. When you quote a person's precise words, put their words in speech marks (' …').

> Halliday (1978, p.1) claims that 'A child creates, first his child tongue, then his mother tongue, in interaction with that little coterie of people who constitute his meaning group.' …

When you quote a person's precise words, put their words in speech marks.

You can either insert this quote into the body text of your writing, as above, or you can use a display quote style, separating it from your body text, placing it on the next line and indenting it, in which case it is usual to omit the speech marks.

Don't let the quote do all the explanatory work. Write in your own words and use the quote as supporting evidence for your argument.

Although quotes can be a good way to add interest to your writing, you must be careful not to rely on them too much. A quote should back up the argument that you yourself are making, it shouldn't make the argument for you.

It is a common mistake to let the quote do all the explanatory work, so remember, write in your own words and use the quote simply as supporting evidence for your argument.

7 Choosing a writing style

The purpose of academic writing is always the same: to take a topic and put forward ideas and reasons that explain it, using words, quotes, statistics, practical examples drawn from experiment or diagrams.

The best guide to how you should express yourself in an assignment is your course materials ... take note of your tutor's feedback on your last assignment.

Academic writing needs to sound more formal, or impersonal, than most other writing styles. However, academic disciplines do vary in the way language is used. So what is expected of you in your writing may differ depending on whether you are doing, for example, a course from an arts or a science discipline. The best guide to how you should express yourself in an assignment is the course materials themselves. Look at your text books and at your assignment handbook.

> ❛ I enjoy writing, but there seems to be a mystique to this kind of 'academic' writing that I can't fathom. ❜

Take note of feedback from your tutor on your previous assignments. Your tutors will give you guidance on how to hone your writing skills for your next assignment.

Make your writing concise by cutting out redundant words.

In some academic writing expressing yourself in the first person is acceptable (e.g., 'I think that …'). However, on most occasions the passive voice (e.g., 'it is thought that …') is preferred as it is more impersonal and objective.

Tips on writing style and expressing yourself well

- Avoid colloquial and idiomatic language.

- Learn to avoid personal pronouns such as 'I', 'we', 'you'.

- Try to use objective language. Useful phrases are: 'It can be argued that ...', rather than 'I think that'.

- Make your writing concise by cutting out redundant words, for example: 'absolutely essential' (just say 'essential'); 'combined together' (just say 'combined'); 'The great majority of' (just say 'the majority of', or even 'most').

- Be aware of specialist terminology. Sometimes words are used in different and very precise ways, for example, the words 'mouse' and 'window' are used in a particular way in computing. In science, 'melting' is not the same as 'dissolving'.

- Use a thesaurus to help you avoid using the same word too often.

- Make sure that your sentences aren't too long, otherwise the reader is likely to lose the thread of your argument. There should be one idea per sentence. If a sentence is too long you may be trying to convey too much information in it.

- Use inverted commas around words or phrases that you use in an unusual or contentious way.

8 Improving your written English

Many students worry about expressing themselves accurately and clearly in assignments. Developing a good writing style sometimes takes years of practice.

8.1 Writing for university

Although academic English is different from everyday written English, the ability to write in an academic style is something that you learn as part of your university study. Don't expect to be able to write in academic English until you have read a number of your course materials, learned some of the terms and begun to write about your subject.

At the beginning of your studies you won't be expected to produce perfectly written assignments. Level 1 courses are geared towards helping you start writing for university and your tutor will help you develop your writing skills.

As you progress through Level 2 and Level 3 courses you will find that greater assignment writing skills are expected of you. You will still be given guidance on writing skills where necessary, however, feedback will concentrate more on the content of your assignment rather than your basic writing skills.

The Skills for OU Study website gives guidance in completing assignments at university level.

8.2 Grammar, spelling and punctuation

There are plenty of helpful resources if you are worried about your grammar and spelling. Find a comprehensive dictionary and thesaurus to help you check spelling and find new words to use – some are available online. The spell check facility in your word processor can be very useful, but do be careful about relying on the spell check unthinkingly as you need to be sure the correct word is in place.

Skills for OU Study includes links to useful websites to help you with spelling and grammar.

8.3 Your tutor and your regional office

Feedback on your assignments will help you to develop your writing skills. Read the comments carefully. They will help you develop your skills in communicating your ideas. Take time to refer back to what you did in the light of the feedback and see whether you can apply that advice to the next assignment. Don't lose marks needlessly by repeating errors that you can easily put right. If you're not sure about any of the comments, or how they affected your marks, ask your tutor for clarification. You could also contact the Learner Support team at your regional centre; they may offer learning skills workshops or even one-to-one sessions to help you improve.